BUSES IN ESSEX IN THE 21ST CENTURY

DAVID MOTH

AMBERLEY

First published 2025

Amberley Publishing
The Hill, Stroud
Gloucestershire, GL5 4EP

www.amberley-books.com

Copyright © David Moth, 2025

The right of David Moth to be identified as
the Author of this work has been asserted in
accordance with the Copyrights, Designs and
Patents Act 1988.

ISBN 978 1 3981 1984 0 (print)
ISBN 978 1 3981 1985 7 (ebook)

British Library Cataloguing in Publication Data.
A catalogue record for this book is available from
the British Library.

Origination by Amberley Publishing.
Printed in the UK.

Introduction

This collection, my eighth to be published by Amberley, concentrates on buses in Essex since the beginning of the twenty-first century. Unlike my book previous to this one, *Perth Buses Since 1990*, which included images contributed by several other bus photographers, it was my intention that this book should strictly feature only photographs taken by me. Well, I was almost successful in the execution of my intention. In its final completed form, the 176 photos in this book were taken by myself; the remaining four, however, were taken by my friend Nigel Utting, though I was with him when he took them.

It was also my intention to keep images that have featured in any of my previous books to a minimum – certainly no more than about eight. Well, not only was I successful in that, but in the end I used no images that have been in previous books.

Being the pedantic person that I am, as far as I'm concerned the twenty-first century commenced on 1 January 2001, so there are no images from 2000 in this book. As it turns out there are also no images from 2001. This was simply because when I went through the candidate images for this book, all the images from 2001 had either featured in a previous book or were of too poor quality. And I was determined this time not to reuse any images from any previous books. So the images featuring in this book commence in 2002 and go right up to June 2023, when I was putting the finishing touches to it.

This has probably been the most difficult book I've completed as I had over 1,600 images to choose from. Fortunately, some of the candidate images could possibly be carried over to a future title, so this helped.

Essex is a surprisingly varied county, ranging from the largely built-up south to the larger towns such as Brentwood, Basildon, Billericay, Braintree, Maldon, Harlow and Clacton to the cities of Southend, Chelmsford and Colchester, all three of which were granted city status during the time period covered by this book, plus the countryside and largely rural north of the county. Obviously while I was taking the vast majority of these photos, I had no idea that one day they would form the basis of a book, which is my excuse for why some places are inevitably underrepresented, such as Harlow, Burnham-on-Crouch, Great Dunmow, etc. Unfortunately a few places aren't featured at all, such as Grays, Stanford-le-Hope, Saffron Walden, Maldon, South Woodham Ferrers, etc.

I've tried hard to keep the proportion of operators, locations and vehicle types representative of their numbers, but it was a difficult balancing act. The largest operator in Essex is First Essex, which is reflected in that just over 50 per cent of images are of this operator. The First Essex fleet was surprisingly varied during the time covered in this book, comprising largely of buses cascaded from other parts of the First empire. Followers of the Essex bus scene will know that First Essex is the successor to former Tilling/National Bus Company operator Eastern National. At the time of writing First Essex were in the process of repainting most of their fleet into the red and green liveries for local and inter-urban routes respectively.

Other operators featured are Arriva, Stephensons, NIBS, Hedingham, etc. Hedingham and Chambers both started the century as well-known and respected independents, but in 2012 both joined the Go Ahead Group and now the distinction between the two companies is pretty much non-existent.

Stephensons in particular have grown tremendously since the turn of the century and have been successful in taking on routes previously abandoned by the 'big three' groups of First, Arriva and Stagecoach in Essex, Suffolk and more recently Cambridgeshire. Stephensons also took over NIBS in 2018.

The one major operator that only makes one appearance in this book is Stagecoach, who hardly operate into Essex at all.

Likewise, I have endeavoured to represent the different towns, cities and villages of Essex fairly, but the choice of locations does probably reflect where I tended to gravitate to, so Chelmsford, Braintree and Colchester are possibly a little overrepresented. For that I can only acknowledge that is the case, but I have made efforts to take and include photos taken at varied locations in these settlements and tried to avoid the trap of only taking photographs at the bus stations.

I do hope that readers enjoy this representation of what the bus scene in the majority of Essex looked like during this period.

David Moth

When new, these First Essex Optare Solos carried branding for the various town routes in Chelmsford. At lunchtime on 26 June 2002, 522 (EO02 NFD) is heading towards the town centre along Rainsford Road on busy route 45 from Writtle to Moulsham Lodge. The 45 was withdrawn in 2022.

On the same day, First Essex Optare Solo 534 (EO02 NFT) is captured in Chelmsford town centre, opposite the Springfield Road Tesco on the 47. At the time of writing the 47 still survives, albeit much altered.

First Essex Mercedes 0709D 2660 (M660 VJN) was still wearing Thamesway colours when seen at Southend bus station on 17 October 2002. This bus was later painted into First livery and transferred to First Hampshire & Dorset, where it was allocated to Hilsea depot.

Arriva Southend Dennis Dominator 5273 (G663 FKA) is captured working service 1 on the dull day of 31 December 2002. This bus was new to North Western as 663 in June 1990 and came to Southend in 1999 after a spell with London & Country.

First Essex Leyland Olympian 4012 (C412 HJN) and Bristol VRT 3219 (WTH 941T) are seen in the interior of Chelmsford's old Tilling Group-style Duke Street bus station on 28 February 2004. 3219 was new to South Wales Transport Company as 941 in 1978 and was working on the 351 and 72 that day as part of the protracted Bristol VR farewell being conducted by First Essex at the time. This bus station was closed within a year and demolished in 2005.

Coach-seated First Essex Leyland Olympian 34814 (C414 HJN) was delivered new to Eastern National in that company's dual-purpose version of the 'spinach and custard' livery, introduced that year in anticipation of deregulation and privatisation. It also wore the Badgerline-style livery for a while before gaining First livery, as seen when I took this photo in 2004 in Chelmsford bus station. This bus was later transferred to Weymouth where it had an extended life, surviving to 2010.

Sunday 5 February 2006 sees Chambers Volvo Olympian S851 DGX loading for a rail replacement working for One Railway, as the franchise was known as at the time. Chambers were obviously taking no chances with tree damage, judging by the metalwork guarding the upper-deck front bulkhead. It was new to Metrobus, which is a little ironic as Metrobus and Chambers would later come under common ownership. In 2009 this bus passed to Harpur's Coaches of Derby, who would put a more conventional tree guard on the nearside of the upper-deck front bulkhead.

First Essex 43731 (S731 TWC) is a low-floor Dennis Dart SLF delivered new to First in 1998 for the new Diamond route between Southend and Bishop's Stortford via Chelmsford and Stansted Airport (the predecessor to the current X30 route). It is seen on layover at Braintree Bus Park on Sunday 16 July 2006. This bus is currently preserved in a version of Eastern National's 'spinach and custard' livery for privatisation, although it never ran like this in service.

Above and below: On a few Sundays in the summer of 2006, Blue Triangle ran free bus services on two routes across Essex using vintage London buses. On 16 July 2006 green Routemaster coach RCL2260 (CUV 260C) is seen opposite The Stag in Hatfield Heath and AEC Regent RT3062 (KXW 171) is at Braintree Bus Park. These buses were obviously lovingly cared for.

First Essex 56008 (EY54 BRX) was a Mercedes 0814D with a coach interior delivered to First Essex for the X30 route between Southend and Stansted Airport. This route has proved to be a tremendous success, reflected in the fact that as time went on the vehicles used to operate it have gradually got bigger, and at the time of writing the route is currently operated by Scania N250UD double-deckers. It is seen calling at Chelmsford railway station on 7 October 2006.

First Essex Dennis Dart 46143 (M943 TEV) was new to Thamesway as 943. It wore Eastern National's yellow with green skirt version of First's 'East Anglia' livery for a while, but by the time I took this photograph of it on 6 July 2007 it was wearing First 'Barbie' livery.

Stansted Transit MAN 14.220 AE08 DLF is seen in the picturesque Essex village of Finchingfield on 17 June 2008.

Hedingham Dennis Dart L351 (EU56 FLM) is seen loading for the rural route 9 in Braintree sometime in 2008. This bus was renumbered to 257 in 2014.

Stansted Transit also had several Dennis Darts with Plaxton bodywork. KV03 ZGP, wearing an all-white livery, is seen in Braintree Bus Park on 22 February 2008.

Another Stansted Transit Dart was EU06 KOX, which was captured at Stansted Airport coach and bus station in March 2008 about to head off to Braintree on the busy 133. This location has changed since, the most significant alteration being the erection of barriers and gates.

Stansted Transit Dennis Dart EU06 KOW is also seen during 2008. After the demise of Stansted Transit, this bus would pass through quite a few different operators

Stansted Transit Alexander Dennis Enviro200 KX57 FMC is seen at rest in Braintree Bus Park in 2008 and was a regular performer on the 133 between Braintree and Stansted Airport.

First Essex Scania L94UB Wright Solar 65690 (YS03 ZKK) is seen in Braintree Bus Park in late 2008, shortly after the bus park was remodelled that year. Prior to this the 70 had terminated in Fairfield Road.

Service 1 was a new route commissioned by Essex County Council and for a few years provided a direct bus route between Writtle to Canvey Island via Chelmsford, East Hanningfield, Battlesbridge and Rayleigh. On 27 June 2008, Regal Busways Dennis Dart/MCV Evolution 701 (AE55 EHM) is seen half poking out of the railway bridge in Duke Street, Chelmsford, while loading for this route. This bus would later pass to Ensignbus as their 785.

New to Maidstone & District in 1988 as their 5891, Leyland Olympian/Northern Counties E891 AKN was transferred by Arriva to Southend in 2004 where it kept the same fleet number. It is seen in the rain at Rayleigh town centre on 12 September 2008.

Two other Leyland Olympians in the Arriva Southend fleet also seen in Rayleigh on the same day are Alexander-bodied 5392 (F572 SMG) and all Leyland 5404 (H264 GEV). 5392 was new to Alder Valley South, while 5404 was new to Southend Transport in 1990 as 264 and spent just over eighteen months with Arriva Colchester before returning in 2004.

Hedingham Bristol VRT L253 (PWY 39W) was new as West Yorkshire 1753 in 1980. It was later with Viscount for six years before spending a further fourteen years with Hedingham, and was one of the last four VRs in that fleet. It is seen at a Clacton-based running day on 7 June 2009.

Seen at Braintree on 6 August 2009 is Hedingham Wright Pathfinder-bodied Dennis Lance SLF L212 (M211 WHJ). I understand that the non-matching fleet and registration numbers are due to a mix up of identities between this and M212 WHJ.

Dennis Dart BU51 REG was captured in Braintree on 6 August 2009 during the brief period that Excel ran the 133, following the collapse of Stansted Transit. The route would soon be transferred within the TGM Group to Network Colchester. TGM Group was taken over by Arriva in 2007, although there was no indication of this on the Network Colchester buses at the time.

First Essex Dennis Dart/Marshall 43678 (R678 MEW) was new to First CentreWest as DML249. It came to First Essex via Central Parking at Bristol Airport, of which First was the majority shareholder at the time. It is seen on a local route in Walton on the Naze in August 2009.

Above and below: On 16 October 2009, TGM Dennis Dart S312 JUA is seen in the London version of TGM's parent company Arriva having been recently transferred to Colchester. It was converted to single door in 2011 and painted into Network Colchester livery.

New to Regal Busways the previous year, Optare Solo 205 (YJ58 CDF) is seen at Rayne Road in Braintree on 16 October 2009. This bus saw further service with McGills of Barrhead.

On the same day, Hedingham Volvo B7RLE L340 (EU05 CLJ) is seen on layover between duties on the 89 to Great Yeldham. This was the only Volvo B7RLE operated by Hedingham.

First Essex Bus Leyland Olympian 34815 (C415 HJN) was looking damn good for a twenty-four-year-old vehicle on 16 October 2009, when leaving Chelmsford bus station on the long established 36 to South Woodham Ferrers.

Essex County Bus was a short-lived operation that rose from the ashes of Stansted Transit. They compete briefly with First Essex on the 42 Chelmsford town service and on the 70 between Braintree and Colchester. T415 OUB was an Optare M920 Solo that was new to Meteor Parking (Pink Elephant), Mayfair, in August 1999. It was sold to Ensign, Purfleet, in March 2010, ending up with AD-Rains of Brinkworth, Wiltshire, in November 2010.

Network Colchester Dennis Dart 411 (S311 JUA) was new to Arriva London South as their DDL11 and was transferred to Colchester during the summer of 2009. It is seen in Braintree Bus Park in the snow on 6 January 2010.

Also seen in the snow on the same day is Flagfinders Optare Solo M850 MX57 CBF operating the free shuttle from the bus park to Freeport Shopping Centre (now known as Braintree Village). This bus passed to Phoenix of Blyth at the end of 2011.

First Essex Dennis Dart 46120 (M920 TEV) is captured here on the long established Chelmsford town service 56 on 29 June 2010. This bus was one of twenty-six similar vehicles new to Thamesway in 1994.

On the same day First Essex Volvo Olympian 34310 (L310 PWR) is seen emerging from under the notorious low bridge in Duke Street in Chelmsford. Since this photo was taken, the road surface here has been raised so no double-deckers are permitted to pass under this bridge.

This was a very unusual working. In July 2010 First Essex Optare Solo 53114 (EO02 NDZ) is seen in Braintree Bus Park on the 70 from Colchester to Chelmsford via Braintree. The 70 was extended from Braintree to Chelmsford the previous year.

First Essex Bristol VRT KOO 790V was semi-preserved by the company in later life and is seen on 3 July 2010 making a guest appearance in service on the 351 from Chelmsford to Brentwood. It wears its original Eastern National fleet number of 3072, as opposed to 3870 which is on its paper identity. Back in the days of the National Bus Company, this bus was in dual-purpose livery and used on limited stop services between Southend and Kings Cross via Basildon.

Above and below: The Dennis Dart SLF/Plaxton Pointer combination was a vehicle that became commonplace throughout Britain for many years. Two First Essex examples are seen in the summer of 2010 in Braintree Bus Park. 42934 (SN05 DZP) was photographed in July while 42932 (SN05 EAP) was captured in August.

Regal Busways Optare Solo 201 (YJ06 YSK) is seen in Braintree Bus Park on 3 August 2010 loading for town service 34A to Bocking. The 34/34A route was an Essex County Council contract that was withdrawn soon after I took this photo.

Not the best of photos due to the poor light, but worth including. Network Colchester Dennis Dart/Caetano Compass 512 (HX51 LRK) is seen in September 2010 wearing route branding for Colchester town service 6, but is seen on layover in Braintree Bus Park in between duties on the 133 to Stansted Airport.

Network Colchester's Dennis Darts were the mainstay of the 133 from 2008 to 2013. On 20 October 2010, 529 (AY54 FRC) is seen passing the White Hart Hotel in the centre of Braintree, looking smart in the standard TGM livery.

Captured on the same occasion is Hedingham Dennis Dart L325 (EX02 RYR) running out of service, also looking well in this operator's much admired traditional livery.

First Essex Dennis Dart 46185 (N985 EHJ) is seen in Brentwood High Street loading for the 551 to Basildon on 23 June 2011, only a couple of months before the end of its service life.

First Essex 43800 (S979 JLM) was a Dennis Dart SLF built as a demonstrator by and for Marshall Coachbuilders of Cambridge in December 1998. It did the rounds with various First subsidiaries up and down the UK before finding a home with First Essex in 2004. It is seen in Brentwood High Street on local route 73 on 23 June 2011.

Arriva Southend Dennis Dart 3387 (P257 FPK) hadn't long been painted into this version of the Arriva livery when I photographed it in Rayleigh on 23 June 2011. It was withdrawn in 2013.

Also seen at Rayleigh station that day was Arriva Southend Dennis Dart 3400 (R310 NGM) in an earlier version of fleet livery. This bus was new to Limebourne in 1997 for route 156 in south London.

In 1997, Eastern National, by then a subsidiary of First Bus, received a batch of Dennis Lances, which were the only buses that EN received new with Northern Counties bodywork. These also turned out to be the last batch of buses delivered in Eastern National livery. 67008 (P508 MNO), which was new as 1508 in 1996, is seen at Osborne Street, Colchester, on 23 June 2011 and was withdrawn the following month.

First Essex Dennis Dart 43436 (P436 NEX) is seen on the seafront in Walton-on-the-Naze on 24 July 2011 loading on service 8 to Clacton. This bus had been acquired from First Eastern Counties earlier in the year, hence the Norwich registration.

First Essex 61054 (R434 GSF) was a Scania L113CRL with a Wright Axcess Ultralow body. It was captured at St Botolph's roundabout by Colchester Town station on 3 September 2011. This bus was new to Rider York, where it was one of the very last buses to not be specified to First Group standards.

Arriva TGM Network Colchester Scania CN94UB Omnicity 2805 (YN53 GGO) was one of a small number that were used on the 133 for a few years. It is seen departing Braintree Bus Park on 14 September 2011. This bus was new to Menzies Aviation, Heathrow. It later spent time with Bay Travel of Cowdenbeath, where it was used on the Forth Road Bridge replacement bus services.

Manufactured in the USA by Georgia-based Blue Bird Corporation, Q275 LBA is a rare and significant survivor formerly operated by the First Group. This prototype vehicle was imported by First Group to demonstrate the 'yellow school bus' concept to the UK government, to persuade them to follow the US method of ensuring that all school buses were dedicated yellow buses. Given fleet number 68000, this prototype vehicle was built to US specification, although was naturally a right-hand drive model for the UK roads. First exhibited it at Showbus in 2001, showcasing the concept to the public.

However, it was soon discovered that this vehicle failed to comply with UK legislation standards for carrying passengers. It was allocated to First Manchester, then transferred to Essex, where it became a familiar sight in Braintree for a while, where it was used to convey staff between the bus park and First's depot in Springwood Estate. The staff seemed to like setting the destination display to different destinations in the southern Greater Manchester area.

There is some irony that the 42, which was introduced in October 1986 as Chelmsford's first minibus route, became the last of Chelmsford's town services to occasionally see double-deckers. On 19 May 2012, just a matter of days before Chelmsford was officially proclaimed a city, Volvo Olympian 34286 (P186 TGD) is seen on Victoria Road South shortly about to pass under the low bridge in Duke Street. This started life with Strathclyde Buses as VO86, and after a spell at Leicester it spent just over ten years with First Essex. The year after I took this photo it was transferred to First Potteries at Newcastle-under-Lyme.

P855 VUS was a Dennis Dart/East Lancs purchased new by Strathclyde Buses' low-cost GCT operation (Comlaw No. 313) as their MD4 in February 1997. It was reputed that this batch was a cancelled order for British Bus-owned London & Country. When Arriva took over BB, East Lancs was owned by BB Chairman Dawson Williams and there were rumours of fraud concerning finance from the Bank of Boston. Arriva were keen to distance themselves from any fall-out and cancelled the order. First Bus picked it up as they needed every vehicle they could muster at the time to repel Stagecoach Glasgow incursions into the city. It found its way into the First Essex fleet in 2002 as fleet number 765 and became 42855 in the 2004 renumbering. It is seen in Braintree on 21 May 2012.

Volvo B7TL 32481 (AU53 HJY) began and ended its long nineteen-year service life with First Eastern Counties, with the First Essex meat in the sandwich occurring between 2011 and 2019. Route branding for Colchester town services 61 and 62 was carried when captured 8 December 2012.

First Essex Dennis Dart 42920 (EU05 AUM) was on the long established Chelmsford local route 56 when I photographed it on Springfield Road in the early afternoon on 10 December 2012. The 56 was about the only Chelmsford town (now city) service still largely doing what it was doing since the 1970s, such as running between North Springfield and North Avenue, albeit much extended at either end.

On the same day, First Essex Optare Solo 53130 (EO02 NFM) is seen calling at the Vineyards in Great Baddow on the cross-Chelmsford city route 40. This route was originally introduced 1978, running from Westlands Estate to Chelmsford High Street. After many alterations over ears, it was withdrawn in 2022.

First Essex Dennis Trident 32810 (T810 LLC) was new as First Capital TN810 and featured roller blinds, but had been transferred to First Essex and fitted with an electronic destination display when I took this photo in Colchester on 5 February 2013. After six years in Essex it departed in 2016 for First Hampshire & Dorset's Southampton depot.

First Essex 34018 (P546EFL) was new to Stagecoach Viscount as part of a large batch of Northern Counties Palatine-bodied Volvo Olympians delivered to the Cambus and Viscount fleets in 1996/97 to replace several dozen Bristol VRTs that were still present in those fleets at the time. Stagecoach decided not to renew the lease on many of these, so these mid-life buses were snapped up by other operators including First. It is seen loading in Colchester in the wet weather of 11 February 2013 for the 75 to Maldon. This bus was withdrawn and scrapped by the end of that year.

Chambers Volvo Olympian S218 YOO was new as Dublin Bus RV417 (98-D-20417) and was re-registered when it was exported to East Anglia. It is seen in Colchester on 11 February 2013. Note the extensive tree guard arrangement on the front upper-deck bulkhead. Chambers had become part of the Go Ahead Group in June 2012.

First Essex Dennis Trident 33088 (LN51 GMU) was new to First Capital in 2002 as TNL1088 working out of Dagenham garage and arrived in Essex at the end of 2012. When I took this photo on 21 February 2013 it was working Braintree town service 30. This service was usually worked by single-deckers.

Arriva Southend Optare Versa 4207 (YJ61 CJO) waits at Shoeburyness East Beach between duties on the 9 to Rayleigh via Eastwood on 14 April 2013. 4207 bounced around various parts of Arriva's south-eastern territory before returning once again to Southend.

TGM Network Colchester Volvo B10BLE 401 (W906 UJM) was captured at St Botolph's roundabout in central Colchester, working service 8 on 23 April 2013. This bus was new to Capital Coaches of Twickenham in 2000 and passed to Tellings-Golden Miller after only nine months when TGM took Capital over. It later received Arriva livery and fleet number 3828 and was transferred to Guildford.

On 2 May 2013, First Essex Optare Solo 53129 (EO02 NFL) was on the short-lived H2 circular service from Broomfield Hospital to Broomfield Hospital via Woodhall Estate, the city centre, Springfield Park and North Springfield. Not long after I took this photo, this route was split. The western part was replaced by an extension of the 40, while the eastern portion reverted back to being the 47.

First Essex 69517 (BJ11 ECN), a Volvo B7RLE/Wright Eclipse Urban 2 painted black for the Chelmsford Park & Ride, is loading in Duke Street for Sandon on 2 May 2013.

First Essex Volvo B7RLE 66817 (MX05 CDZ) and Volvo Olympian 34305 (L305 PWR) are seen in Duke Street, passing Chelmsford railway station, which was undergoing rebuilding at the time. It was very shortly after I took this photo on 21 July 2014 that the road surface under the bridge was raised, so all double-deckers are barred from going under this bridge now.

First Essex Volvo Olympian 34307 (L307 PWR) is seen in Colchester in 2014, looking a bit scruffy as it was nearing the end of its life. This bus was new to Yorkshire Rider in 1994 and was transferred to First Essex four years later.

Hedingham Volvo B10B 480 (S376MVP) started life as a Volvo Bus demonstrator before being acquired during 1999, and is seen laying over in the familiar surroundings of Braintree Bus Park on 27 August 2014. The fleet renumbering at the start of 2014 saw the demise of the attractive traditional style of fleet numbers, as well as 480's previous identity of L301.

On the same day, Network Colchester Volvo B7RLE 3825 (GN07 AVO) is seen in Braintree Bus Park on the 133 between Colchester and Stansted Airport. These buses carried route branding for the 133 and had very comfortable seats, making them very suitable for this long route.

Regal Busways Trident 1401 (V761 HBY) was captured in Braintree on 20 March 2015, working the free shuttle bus service to Braintree Freeport. This bus was new to Metroline as TP61 and was subsequently written off by fire on 12 December 2014 on the A12.

Also in Braintree Bus Park on that day was Stephensons Alexander Dennis Enviro200 423 (EU64 DVT) working rural service 9 to Great Bardfield.

First Essex Dennis Enviro200 44539 (YX13 AHO) is turning out of Arbour Lane onto Springfield Road on its way to North Melbourne via Chelmsford city centre on the long established cross-city 56 from Springfield to Melbourne on 8 July 2015. This bus has subsequently acquired branding for Brentwood town service 37.

Stephensons Alexander Dennis Enviro200 431 (EU10 NVP) catches the late afternoon sun of 12 October 2015 as it loads outside Witham station for the 90 to Maldon, for which it carried route branding.

Two Hedingham Volvo Olympians are seen in the village of Tollesbury, approaching the end of their lives on 12 October 2015. On the left is Northern Counties 72 (R629 MNU), while on the right with Alexander R-type bodywork is 74 (R702 DNH). Before renumbering at the start of 2014 these were L373 and L384 in the fleet. (Nigel Utting)

On the same day, standing outside the now sadly closed and demolished Tollesbury bus depot, is Hedingham Dennis Dart 259 (EU56 FLP). This depot was the former base of the long established local independent Osborne's, who Hedingham took over in 1997. (Nigel Utting)

Unfortunately I don't know the date of this photograph, though Dennis Dart 46183 (N983 EHJ) was disposed of in 2013. This was one of the very last surviving buses in the First Essex fleet with a step entrance and was captured by me in Braintree Bus Park. I believe it was being used to shuttle staff to and from the bus depot that day.

Now in Arriva livery, Volvo B7RLE 3825 (GN07 AVO) makes a second appearance in this book. It is seen in Braintree Bus Park on 31 October 2016 on its usual haunt, the 133.

First Essex Volvo B7TL/Wright Eclipse Gemini 32642 (KP54 AZD) lays over in Braintree on 28 April 2017. This bus was a transfer from First Leicester at the start of 2014.

First Essex Volvo 7900 hybrid 69918 (BV13 ZCA) is seen departing Chelmsford bus station while still in original colours on 30 May 2017, not long before being repainted into the new 100 dedicated 2017 livery.

Stephensons Dennis Dart 409 (GU52 HKD) was looking very smart when I took this photo of it while it was on layover in Braintree Bus Park on 13 June 2017.

On 15 July 2017 First Essex Scania L94UB 62409 (YS03 ZKD) is seen in Osborne Street, Colchester, setting off to Chelmsford on the normally double-decker worked 70 to Chelmsford via Braintree. (Nigel Utting)

First Essex Volvo B7RLE 66811 (MX05 CDK) sets off from Burnham-on-Crouch in the fading light of 15 July 2017 on the lengthy 31X to Chelmsford via Maldon, Danbury and Great Baddow bypass. (Nigel Utting)

By the time I took this photo, First Essex were using new buses on the Chelmsford Park & Ride. On 12 August 2017, First Essex Dennis Enviro200 MMC 67196 (SN66 WKT) was captured in New Street in Chelmsford on the P&R to Sandon.

On 15 September 2017, First Essex Alexander Dennis Enviro200 MMC 67164 (YY66 PBF) is at Chelmsford bus station, loading for the X10 limited stop service for Stansted Airport. Since this photo was taken, a barrier has been erected alongside the pavement.

Regal Busways Dennis Dart SLF 618 (NA52 AWF) was new to Go Wear Buses in December 2002. It later passed to Western Greyhound of Newquay prior to passing into Regal's hands before operating briefly with A2B Bus & Coach of Cambridge. I took this photo of it on 21 September 2017.

First Essex Optare Solo 53126 (EO02 NFH) outside Chelmsford railway station, wearing the new First livery on 22 September 2017. When new in 2002 with fleet number 526, it wore route branding for the 45. It was scrapped the following year.

At the same location on the same day was First Essex Dennis Dart 42931 (SN05 EAO) still wearing First's 'Barbie' livery.

Just two months old, Arriva Colchester Wrightbus Streetlite 4324 (SK68 TWV) sits at Braintree Bus Park on New Year's Day 2019. This bus, along with its sister 4323, were delivered in this attractive Arriva Sapphire livery with route branding for the 133.

Volvo B10BLE 66179 (W379 EOW) was new to First Hampshire's Hilsea depot in 2000. It came to First Essex in 2011 after a three-year spell with First Eastern Counties. When I took this photograph in Braintree Bus Park on 9 January 2019 it was working as a driver training vehicle.

First Essex Volvo B9TL/Wright Gemini 37138 (SN57 HCX) was new to First Edinburgh in November 2007. After transfer to Midland Bluebird in 2014 it gained a special livery for the X62 Edinburgh–Peebles route, before coming to First Essex three years later when it was painted into this version of First livery, incorporating branding for the 62/A/B group of routes to Brightlingsea. It was captured in the early afternoon sun on 21 May 2019.

On the same day, I took this photo of Hedingham Alexander Dennis Enviro200 265 (EU10 AOX). It was still painted in the company's traditional and attractive cream and red fleet livery in which it was delivered.

New to Connex of Jersey as 1178 (J 52083), this Alexander Dennis Enviro200 became First Essex 44596 (EU60 LFS) in 2013, and is seen entering Chelmsford bus station on 1 June 2019 on the recently introduced service 57 between the city centre and North Springfield. This utilised the Chelmer Valley inner relief road, therefore giving the residents of North Springfield a much faster journey to the city centre than the existing 54 and 56, which continued to run alongside the new route.

Wearing the new livery introduced for Hedingham and Chambers buses, Hedingham Volvo B7TL 514 (LB02 YXF) departs Braintree Bus Park for the railway station on 25 June 2019 on the 89 from Great Yeldham. This bus was new as East Thames Buses VWL8, coming to Hedingham via Konectbus after spells with London General and London Central.

Stephensons Transbus Dart SLF/Pointer 2 403 (EU03 CFX) is seen on 22 July 2019 in Braintree on local service 21, which the company introduced to partially replace the route withdrawn by First Essex after their closure of Braintree depot.

Scania N94UD/East Lancs OmniDekka 637 (YN55 NJE) basks in the sun while on layover in Braintree Bus Park on 7 August 2019. This bus was new to Transdev London Sovereign as their SLE27 and entered service with Stephensons in 2014 after conversion to single-door.

First Essex Alexander Dennis Enviro350H hybrid 67904 (SN13 CHY) is seen in Braintree Bus Park on 7 August 2019 on the 42B. This was an extension of Chelmsford city service 42 and was introduced to dovetail with the 70, providing a bus every fifteen minutes during the daytime between Chelmsford and Braintree.

Volvo B7RLE/Wright Eclipse Urban 66814 (MX05 CDU) is seen on the same day, also in Braintree Bus Park, which was in its final few months of existence. It would close the following year to be rebuilt and replaced by the new Braintree Bus Interchange.

First Essex Volvo B9TL 37985 (BJ11 XGY) was new to First Hampshire & Dorset at Portsmouth, then was used by First Berkshire for a while on the 702 between London and Windsor, for which it wore Green Line branding. It makes its first appearance in this book, departing Chelmsford bus station on 9 August 2019 on the X30 Stansted Airport to Southend, for which it was painted in a special livery.

On the same day, I took this photo of First Essex 44661 (YX66 WBF), one of the many smaller Alexander Dennis Enviro200 MMCs that operate in the city on local routes, whilst calling at the railway station on the 57, which had recently been extended to Galleywood via Great Baddow over roads previously served by the 40.

Lodge Coaches DAF SB220/Wrights F20 DGE was new to Fishwick's of Leyland as YJ03 PFF and is typical of their well-kept fleet. It is seen arriving into Chelmsford on the market days only route from Great Dunmow to Chelmsford via The Easters on 9 August 2019.

Also in Chelmsford on that day was First Essex Volvo 7900 hybrid 69916 (BV13 ZBY), where it is seen about to depart the bus station on the lengthy route 100 to Lakeside via Billericay, Basildon, Stanford-le-Hope and Grays.

First Essex Dennis Dart 42931 (SN05 EAO) makes its second appearance in this book, this time on 29 August 2019. By this time it had been repainted into the new First 'Olympia' livery. Again it is seen loading outside Chelmsford railway station.

First Essex Volvo B7TLs 37010 (WX55 VHV) and 32640 (KP54 AZB) pause in a top and tail fashion in Coggeshall on 31 August 2019 while performing opposite workings on Colchester–Chelmsford service 70.

Above and below: Two photos of Stephensons Alexander Dennis Enviro200s 476 (EU65 EOM) and 471 (EU65 EOG) taken at Braintree Bus Park on 23 September 2019. Both wear branding for the 38/38A, which was introduced by Stephensons to replace the 132 between Witham and Halstead, withdrawn by First. It is sobering to realise that the backdrop to these two photos would be swept away within a year of them being taken.

Also on 23 September 2019 over at Southend-on-Sea is First Essex Dennis Trident/Plaxton President 33191 (LT52 XAB). This heritage livery commemorates Westcliff-on-Sea Motor Services, who operated in the area until being absorbed into Eastern National in 1955.

First Essex Alexander Dennis Enviro200 MMC 67160 (YY66 OZV) makes its first appearance in this book, seen on the X10, which was its usual haunt at the time, alongside the newly erected barrier opposite Chelmsford bus station on 9 October 2019.

On 18 October 2019, Maldon-based Arrow Taxis Mercedes 516Cdi AY17 UVM is seen passing Chelmsford station on the infrequent village service 10, which replaced the 52 between Pleshey and West Hanningfield.

Scania L94 65679 (YR52 VEH) was new to Menzies Aviation at Heathrow and spent a short spell with Brighton and Hove before joining First Essex. 65679 is seen at Osborne Street, Colchester, on 2 February 2020, shortly before being sold on to Dan's Coach Travel of Great Finborough.

Possibly looking a bit out of place in a book about Essex buses, Stagecoach London Alexander Dennis Enviro400 MMC 10335 (SN16 OKT) is seen in Brentwood town centre on Transport for London route 498 on 4 February 2020. The 498 was introduced to replace the section of the 351 between Brentwood and Romford withdrawn by First Essex.

Also in Brentwood that day was NIBS Dennis Dart 458 (SN55 DVR). NIBS was taken over by Stephensons in 2018 and that is reflected in the Stephensons-style fleet number. This bus was new to National Car Parks and came to NIBS via London United. It was later sold to Herbert's Travel of Blunham.

Seen at Basildon bus station on 11 February 2020 is First Essex 41524 (LK03 UFB), a Caetano Nimbus-bodied 10.2-metre Transbus Dart SLF based at Basildon depot, working route 8 to Pitsea Broadway. This was new as First Capital DHL524, being renumbered to DMC41524 very early in its life.

First Essex Alexander Dennis Enviro200 MMC 67161 (YY66 OZW) departs Basildon bus station on the same day. Despite wearing branding for the X10, it was on the 100 from Chelmsford to Lakeside.

First Essex Volvo 7900H 69906 (BV13 ZBJ) is seen at Chelmsford bus station on its usual haunt, the 100. This photo was taken on 24 June 2020 during the height of the Covid pandemic, which is reflected by how deserted the scene is and how the entrance to The Original Plough is gated closed.

New to Go Goodwins of Eccles and given the name *Carol*, Stephensons Alexander Dennis Enviro200 426 (MX62 APO) is seen on Fairfield Road in Braintree on 26 June 2020. The closure of Braintree Bus Park in April 2020 meant that several temporary bus stops were put into use on the surrounding streets, including this one.

First Essex Transbus Trident/ALX400 33376 (LK53 EYV) was new to First Centrewest as TNA33376. It migrated east to First Essex at Hadleigh after a short spell with First Games Transport for the 2012 London Olympic Games. It is seen at Southend Victoria railway station on 13 July 2020.

First Essex Dennis Dart 42933 (SN05 DZO) catches the afternoon sun on 20 July 2020 as it pauses in Springfield Road, Chelmsford, on the cross-city 54 from Springfield to North Melbourne. This bus was new to First Devon & Cornwall.

First Essex Alexander Dennis Enviro200 44001 (LK57 EJD) calls at Southend Victoria on 9 August 2020. It is interesting to compare the contrasting architectural styles of the buildings in the background on either side of the bus.

At the same location that day was Wrightbus Streetlite 63167 (SN64 CJO). Note the sticker showing support for the NHS staff during the Covid pandemic.

First Essex Dennis Dart 42927 (SN05 EAF) had just arrived in Chelmsford bus station on the 71 from Colchester when I took this photo on 10 August 2020. Life was gradually making some sort of return to normality after the first lockdown, as can be seen by the fact that The Original Plough is open. It is probably not unfair to say that the Plaxton Pointer body was beginning to look a bit dated when seen amongst newer designs by this time.

New as First Capital DML521, Dennis Dart/Caetano Nimbus (LK03 UEY) was reinstated after being withdrawn for scrap by First Potteries and transferred to First Essex as 41521. After a period in normal service based at Hadleigh, it was painted into this pink livery and was used on staff shuttles and publicity work. It is seen sitting in Duke Street opposite Chelmsford bus station on 11 August 2020.

MK44 3NAolvo B7RLE 66810 (MX05 CDF) was new to First Manchester's Oldham depot in 2005 and moved south to Essex three years later. At the time I took this photo on 11 August 2020 it was based at Colchester and carried local branding.

Also in Colchester that day on Stanwell Street was Hedingham Volvo B7TL 525 (LX05 EZH), new to Go Ahead London General in 2005 as WVL211. Still wearing London red having been acquired in 2018, it is loading for the X76 to Clacton.

Stephensons Alexander Dennis Enviro200 MMC 467 (YX66 WKF) is seen on 12 August 2020 negotiating its way out of Braintree High Street past some Covid signs. This was just before the High Street was closed for pedestrianisation. This bus came to Stephensons of Essex from Stephensons of Easingwold in 2018. Despite the name the two concerns are unrelated.

First Essex Dennis Dart SLF/Plaxton 42932 (SN05 EAP) makes its second appearance in this book. I took this photo of it outside Chelmsford railway station on 17 September 2020. By this time it had been painted into the new livery.

First Essex Volvo B9TL/Wright Gemini 2 37986 (BJ11 ECY) looks particularly superb wearing Eastern National X10 heritage coach livery complete with period-style depot code and fleet number plate when captured on 19 September 2020.

One of a number of former First London Enviro200s in service with First Essex, 44081 (YX58 HVL) approaches Southend bus station on 19 September 2020.

Also in Southend that day was Arriva Southend Enviro400 MMC 6511 (SN66 WJG). This was the first one painted in-house at Gillingham, previous E400 MMC repaints had been by Marden Commercials or ADL Harlow. This batch was introduced in 2016 to upgrade service 1 between Shoeburyness and Rayleigh via Southend, London Road, Hadleigh Church and Thundersley Kenneth Road.

On 4 December 2020, with a smattering of snow on the roofs of the buildings behind, Stephensons Alexander Dennis Enviro200 469 (SN66 WLL) sits in Manor Street, Braintree, sporting the revised Stephensons fleet name.

First Essex Alexander Dennis Enviro200 44545 (YX13 AKG) calls at Wickford station on 27 April 2021, alongside similar Stephensons 424 (EU15 AZT).

Also in Wickford that day was slightly older Alexander Dennis Enviro200 44910 (YX09 AFZ), which has a capacity of twenty-eight seats compared to the thirty-nine of 44545 above.

New to First Halifax and transferred to First Essex four months previously, Volvo B7TL 32531 (YJ54 XUY) is seen approaching Southend Victoria on 27 April 2021. Note the large sticker across the upper-deck windows encouraging customers to use contactless payment. This was very much a message that the bus-operating industry was keen to get across during the pandemic and after.

In Rayleigh on the same day is First Essex Alexander Dennis Enviro400 33567 (SN58 CHG). The 'Sorry bus full, Social distancing' display is a sign of the time in which this photo was taken. It was on the 25 to Southend at the time.

On 27 April 2021 I took this photo of Stephensons Alexander Dennis Enviro200 424 (EU15 AZT) while it was catching some rays at the bus stands next to Wickford railway station. It still had the old style of company fleet name, which was slowly being replaced by the new version at the time.

First Essex Alexander Dennis Enviro200 44540 (YX13 AHP) had just arrived in Chelmsford on the 32 from Ongar, despite wearing route branding for Brentwood town service 37. This was in the in the late afternoon of 4 May 2021 in Duke Street.

First Essex Volvo B7RLE 69520 (BJ11 ECW) is resplendent in heritage Thamesway livery depicting an era that seems recent, but at the same time is maybe longer ago than would generally be realised. It is seen on 10 May 2021 at Hadleigh Church. At the time of writing it had recently been transferred to Colchester.

Though not actually wearing a heritage livery here, the rarity of surviving buses still dressed like this at this time did make it resemble one. This was one of three Dennis Tridents transferred from First Midland Red in December 2020 and still looked good in First's Barbie scheme. First Essex 33403 (VX54 MTZ) is seen opposite Rayleigh station on 10 May 2021.

Hedingham Dennis Dart 254 (EU05 AUR) was new as L339 in March 2005 and still retained its original livery in this view in Clacton on 12 May 2021. It was the first of seven Dart SLFs bought new while the company was still proudly independent, this first pair being the less common 10.5-metre length. It was withdrawn the following year.

First Essex Wright Streetlite 47655 (SN15 AEV) is seen in Billericay town centre on 27 May 2021. Later that year, a Christmas livery would be applied to this bus.

First Essex Volvo B9TL 36218 (BJ12 VXB) was waiting to return to Hullbridge on service 20 when captured in Southend on 28 May 2021.

First Essex Volvo B9TL 37985 (BJ11 XGY) makes another appearance in this book, this time on 28 May 2021. It received Westcliff-on-Sea heritage livery in 2020 and ultimately replaced 33191 (LT52 XAB) in this role.

NIBS Alexander Dennis Enviro200 419 (CN11 FBE) is seen departing Basildon bus station on 1 June 2021. NIBS have built up quite a presence around Basildon, Billericay, Brentwood and Grays.

On the same day NIBS Scania N270UD/Optare Olympus 515 (EU59 BFK) departs Basildon bus station. NIBS were taken over by Stephensons in October 2018, which is reflected in the Stephensons-style fleet numbers.

Former Go Ahead London (Docklands) SOC7, Scania N230UD 527 (LX08 ECV) looks clean and neat in its new NIBS livery as it departs Basildon bus station, also on 1 June 2021.

On the same day, First Essex Volvo B7TL 32532 (YJ05 VUY) is seen turning into Basildon bus station. This bus was acquired from First West Yorkshire in 2020 and was transferred to Colchester at the end of 2021.

33232 (LT52 WXK), one of the later First Essex Dennis Tridents new to First London, is seen at the bus stop opposite Rayleigh station on 15 June 2021. This was the only gasket-glazed/short wheelbase example at Hadleigh, and was withdrawn the following year.

Stephensons local Brentwood route 71C was withdrawn at the end of April 2021 with the end of developer funding. The regular vehicle used on the route was Mercedes Sprinter 516CDi 301 (RE66 VPD). This bus was used for a few weeks on the 9 between Great Bardfield and Great Notley, on which it is seen turning out of Fairfield Road into South Street, Braintree, on 16 July 2021. It was sold the following year to Taw and Torridge of Barnstaple.

Hedingham Volvo B7TL 510 (LB02 YWX) was still in Konectbus livery when I took this photo of it in Braintree on 21 September 2021, despite having been transferred within the Go Ahead Group two years previously. This was new to East Thames Buses as VWL1.

First Essex Alexander Dennis Enviro200 MMC 67160 (YY66 OZV) stands outside Chelmsford railway station on 11 November 2021, having been recently painted in the new green livery for inter-urban routes, although when captured it was working on the Chelmsford city route C1 (essentially the old 42). Luggage racks are clearly visible from its time allocated to the X10 to Stansted Airport.

Ipswich Buses Scania N94UD/East Lancs Omnidekka 60 (PJ54 YZT) was in Colchester on 17 November 2021 nearing the end of its journey from its hometown on the 93. This route is operated under contract to Suffolk County Council.

First Essex 32068 (KP51 VZS) was one of only two ALX400-bodied Volvo B7TLs left at Colchester depot when viewed at Wivenhoe on 11 January 2022. The other remaining example was 32087 (KP51 WBZ), both having originated with Leicester Citybus twenty years previously.

First Essex Volvo B7TL 37007 (WX55 VHR) carries yet another excellent heritage livery, this time depicting 1990s Badgerline-style Eastern National, albeit minus the badger behind the rear wheels. This was at the new Braintree Interchange on 11 February 2022.

This was an unusual working which I witnessed by sheer chance. Stephensons Scania N94UD/ East Lancs OmniDekka 645 (YN55 NKH) was departing Stansted Airport coach and bus station on 7 May 2022 on local route 5 to Bishop's Stortford. This was normally worked by single-deckers.

Seven new Scania N250UDs arrived at First Essex in late 2019 to upgrade the X30. This batch were the first brand-new double-deckers delivered to Eastern National and its successors since a small batch of three long wheelbase Leyland Olympian coaches in 1986. On 20 May 2022 36837 (YN69 XXU) is seen turning into Coval Lane shortly after departing Chelmsford bus station on its way to Southend. They did also stray occasionally onto the 70 to Colchester via Braintree for a while, although that ceased shortly before the 70 was renumbered 370. They certainly are handsome vehicles.

Hedingham Volvo B7TL 513 (LB02 YXE) departs Braintree Interchange on 9 June 2022 on the last leg of its long journey from Great Yeldham to Braintree railway station. This bus was new to East Thames Buses as VWL7 and came to Hedingham via Konectbus.

Service 350 was introduced in summer 2022 to serve the east of Ingatestone as a temporary measure while gas pipe renewal works were undertaken in the village. During this time the main 351 route bypassed the area by using the A12. First Essex Dennis Dart 42934 (SN05 DZP) is seen calling at Chelmsford railway station on 4 August 2022.

While First Essex are rightly lauded for their efforts in bringing heritage liveries to the streets, Arriva Southend also had a couple of buses that looked great in Southend Transport livery. Volvo B7RLE 3816 (GN07 AVC) looks very smart as it arrives in Southend at the end of the long service 1 from Rayleigh via Hadleigh on 5 August 2022.

New to Yourbus of Heanor and acquired by Stephensons after the collapse of that company, Stephensons Alexander Dennis Enviro200 470 (SN66 WLO) is seen in Southchurch Road in Southend on 5 August 2022.

On the same day at the same location is Arriva Southend Alexander Dennis Enviro400 6500 (SN66 WHT) wearing the new Arriva livery, on the newly introduced 2, which took over the eastern part of the 1 between Southend and Shoeburyness. Service 1 reverted to running between Southend and Rayleigh only.

First Essex 63061 (SK63 KKB) was one of a few Wrightbus Streetlites that found their way over to Essex following the closure of First Hampshire & Dorset's Southampton operations. It was briefly operated by Colchester depot before being transferred to Hadleigh. It is seen in Southend on 5 August 2022 shortly after receiving a repaint into the First Essex green livery.

Arriva Volvo B7RLE 3889 (BG59 FWP) is seen at the Chelmsford Anglia Ruskin University terminus of the 59 from Harlow on 18 August 2022. This old Eastern National route is the only Arriva route to reach Chelmsford.

Snow is clearly visible on Chelmsford railway station behind First Essex Alexander Dennis Enviro200 MMC 67172 (YY66 OZX) in this photo taken in winter sunshine on 14 December 2022.

Seven years on from the previous view in this book, Hedingham Dennis Dart 259 (EU56 FLP) was snapped at Wethersfield on 10 February 2023. Hedingham's buses were due to all have their 'Covid masks' removed by this time, but as can be seen 259 still retained its one.

First Essex 33414 (WA56 FTK) is seen in Chelmsford bus station about to depart to Basildon on the recently introduced 300 on 13 April 2023. The 300 was introduced to replace the northern half of the 100 between Chelmsford and Basildon. Not long after it was introduced it was converted to a double-decker. The previous generation of double-deckers allocated to the route between Chelmsford and Basildon were Bristol FLFs.

First Essex Volvo B7RLE 69431 (AU58 FFT) gives a very pleasing appearance amidst the greenery on Broomfield Road, Chelmsford, on 19 April 2023 wearing the new livery. I do like this new livery, though of course I will admit to being absolutely biased as green is my favourite colour.

In 2022 as part of some extensive route changes, the 70 was renumbered 370. First Essex Volvo B7TL 37133 (SN57 HDH) sports a somewhat brash advertising livery promoting Colchester Zoo and is nearing the end of its journey from Colchester on 4 May 2023, as it negotiates the Parkway/Broomfield Road gyratory in Chelmsford.

The next one around the block is First Essex Wrightbus Streetlite 47601 (SN14 FFG), another recent arrival from Southampton. It has recently been painted into red 'Shuttles' livery for local services.

Above and below: Contrasting First Essex Alexander Dennis Enviro400s viewed on 9 May 2023. 33561 (SN58 CGX) is wearing First Olympia livery and 33424 (VT59 JPT) is wearing heritage livery, which recreates National Bus Company 'leaf green' as worn by Eastern National buses over a period of nearly twenty years. 33424, amongst other buses, had been spruced up specially for the Eastern National Heritage Bus Display, which took place the previous day, including painting the wheels and blacking the tyres. They're seen in Billericay and they're doing very well.

Atlas-bodied Mercedes-Benz (RX67 OPU) belonging to Arrow Taxis of Maldon is seen in Billericay High Street on 9 May 2023, some six months after they had secured the contract for service 12 (Billericay to Wickford) in November 2022.

On 14 May 2023 First Essex Alexander Dennis Enviro200 44473 (YX62 BNU) arrives in Chelmsford bus station at the end of its journey on the 351 from Brentwood. This bus was new to Whitelaw of Stonehouse in Scotland, then was with Halton Transport of Widnes until their demise in 2020, after which it found its way to its present owner.

Stephensons Scania N230UD 604 (EU13 EBL) is seen in Southend city centre on what seemed to be its usual haunt of service 60 out to Canewdon and Paglesham on 16 May 2023.

On the same day, First Essex Alexander Dennis Enviro400 MMC 33985 (SN65 OGA) is seen departing Basildon bus station on the 300 to Chelmsford. This was one of a few E400 MMCs that have found their way south from Glasgow, where this one wore route branding for express routes 85 and 87, remnants of which are visible here.

First Essex Alexander Dennis Enviro200 MMC 44661 (YX66 WBF) is seen during lunchtime on 2 June 2023 in Duke Street in Chelmsford city centre. It hadn't long been painted into the red 'Shuttles' livery intended for use by buses on local routes. The C9 is essentially derived from the 57 under the previous numbering scheme, which makes use of the Chelmer Valley Road to give residents of North Springfield and the huge Beaulieu development a fast route to the railway station and city centre.

The distinction between Hedingham and Chambers has got very blurred over the last few years, and now buses are beginning to appear wearing this combined 'Hedingham & Chambers' fleet name. Scania CN230UB Omnicity 462 (NK62 KJN) hadn't long been repainted by Marden Commercials when captured at Clacton railway station on 8 June 2023.

First Essex Volvo B7TL 32669 (SN55 HDZ) was transferred from the West of England fleet in 2020, though remained in its previous two-tone First Scotland livery when seen at Wivenhoe station on 8 June 2023. It spent some of the intervening period after its transfer wearing a vinyl all-over advert for the new branch of Halfords in Colchester.

Ipswich Buses Ltd Alexander Dennis Enviro200 106 (YX66 WCK) is seen pulling out of Colchester Road in Manningtree, on a late afternoon working of the 93 from Colchester to Ipswich on 20 July 2024. The majority of journeys on this service are worked by double-deckers.

First Essex 47665 (SN15 ACF) was one of several Wright Streetlites transferred to Essex. Most were quickly painted into the new red livery for First Essex local services, but when I took this photo in Colchester on 17 June 2023, it was one of four based there which were still wearing their City Red branding for Southampton routes.

The final photograph in this book is of Central Connect Alexander Dennis Enviro200 MMC (CC71 GAL) departing Braintree Interchange on 19 June 2023 on the rural service 9 to Great Bardfield via Shalford and Finchingfield. Central Connect had recently won a few contracts for rural routes around northern Essex.